Catherine McBride's story began in a village at the bottom of a mountain in Northern Ireland. There were further chapters in Pembrokeshire and North Cyprus. She is an explorer and relishes travelling. Colour is a constant motivator. Catherine paints watercolours with a big brush, makes artefacts and loves spontaneity.

The Skylark is her first book and the poems were inspired by her watercolours, which appeared in meditation.

THE SKYLARK

CATHERINE MCBRIDE

Austin Macauley Publishers
LONDON · CAMBRIDGE · NEW YORK · SHARJAH

Copyright © Catherine McBride 2022

The right of **Catherine McBride** to be identified as author of this work has been asserted by the author in accordance with sections 77 and 78 of the Copyright, Designs and Patents Act 1988.

All rights reserved. No part of this publication may be reproduced, stored in a retrieval system, or transmitted in any form or by any means, electronic, mechanical, photocopying, recording, or otherwise, without the prior permission of the publishers.

Any person who commits any unauthorised act in relation to this publication may be liable to criminal prosecution and civil claims for damages.

A CIP catalogue record for this title is available from the British Library.

ISBN 9781398458413 (Paperback)
ISBN 9781398458420 (Hardback)
ISBN 9781398458437 (ePub e-book)

www.austinmacauley.com

First Published 2022
Austin Macauley Publishers Ltd®
1 Canada Square
Canary Wharf
London
E14 5AA

For Rachel and Simon

This world is our home
But we vandalise it, why?
We might all perish.

A fire is blindly
Sweeping through the forest
floor Indiscriminately.

Pity the skylark
She is petrified with fear,
We should grieve for her.

She has sent a plea,
Flying higher and higher
Praying for guidance.

A purple herald,
Spiralling towards the skies.
Her emissary.

The small plaintiff cry
Went viral and amplified,
"Our future is grave."

"Breath of life's being
Help us, save us from
this plight,
Spirit of awareness"

The cry was ignored
By everyone down on earth
They just didn't hear.

Why must we bear these
Immoral codes of conduct
Bolstered up by greed?

Shame, the human race
Depends far too much
on hope.
Pity our folly.

Our hope that reason
And good judgement
will prevail.
Delusional faith

And fires continue
To rage their relentless race.
Burning all in front.

Our trees, our life's blood
Will it be too late for us?
Starved of oxygen.

Watch the egotists
They plunder the earth
they own.
Self-serving raiders.

Wake up from your sleep
Put aside all your grasping ways,
Sound the alarm.

Nature's laws at work
The end and then the beginning.
Carbonisation.

Charred skeletons
Left in testament of death
incineration

Our resignation
In accepting our avarice is
Self-abnegation.

Brothers and sisters
Children of being, take care
We are not separate.

This experience
It's for us, in its abundance
We perceive it.

We are one conscious
Our deeds affect the balance,
Our equilibrium.

If we are in lack
It's what we have manifested
A story we tell.

Temper your ego
It has singular intent
An unruly child.

Be in gratitude
Measure blessings as
your wealth
Be thankful, always.

Marvel at nature
It is exclusively ours
Given in pure love.

God is perfect love
The essence of our spirit.
Have it in your heart

It was with this love
That the skylark was rescued
Saved by cosmic power.

The plea was honoured
Angels of the universe
Valued the prayer

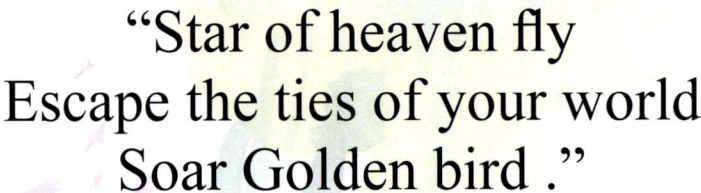

"Star of heaven fly
Escape the ties of your world
Soar Golden bird."

And so it was saved.
The Spirit of Awareness
Rescued the skylark.

The little song bird
Sailed away in a balloon
Now sing, passerine.

Silence, think of that
What if there was no
bird song?
Just dead air, no sound.

Hushed as in death, scorched,
Our life giving trees are gone
Fired and petrified.